S TERRARUM DESCRIPTIO MAGNA

doctorum virorum obfervationib' duobus planifphærijs delineata

This journal belongs to:

Travel &
Adventure
Journal

TRAVEL & ADVENTURE JOURNAL

A place to write about your
hiking, biking, thinking,
canoeing, climbing, dreaming,
snorkeling, camping, traveling,
exploring adventures

NATIONAL
GEOGRAPHIC
SOCIETY
Washington, D.C.

The world's largest nonprofit scientific and educational organization, the National Geographic Society was founded in 1888 "for the increase and diffusion of geographic knowledge." Since then it has supported scientific exploration and spread information to its more than eight million members worldwide. The National Geographic Society educates and inspires millions every day through magazines, books, television programs, videos, maps and atlases, research grants, the National Geographic Bee, teacher workshops, and innovative classroom materials. The Society is supported through membership dues, charitable donations, and income from the sale of its educational products. Members receive NATIONAL GEOGRAPHIC magazine— the Society's official journal—discounts on Society products and other benefits. For more information about the National Geographic Society, its educational programs and publications, and ways to help the Society, please call 1-800-NGS-LINE (647-5463) or write to the following address:

NATIONAL GEOGRAPHIC SOCIETY
1145 17th Street N.W.
Washington, D.C. 20036-4688
U.S.A.

Visit the Society's Web site at www.nationalgeographic.com

Printed in Spain
ISBN 0-7922-8226-4

Cover: An adventurer and a very enlarged photograph of the skin of a living giraffe

Endpapers: A 1669 world map

Opposite the Title Page: A stone face on an abandoned temple at Angkor in Cambodia

Contents Page: Camels in the Sahara

Opposite the Introduction: Sylvia Earle in the 1,000-pound Jim diving suit, which was named for Jim Jarrett, the first person willing to try it.

Page 90: The entrance to the tomb of the Pharaoh Ramses II

Page 100: The Khumbu Icefall on the south side of Mount Everest

Page 114: A sign near Faith, South Dakota, where the largest and one of the most complete *Tyrannosaurus rex* fossils was found

WHAT'S INSIDE

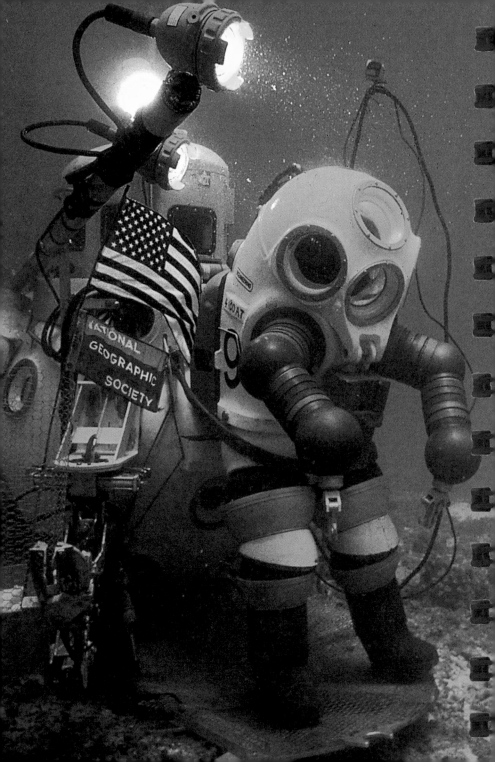

How About an Adventure?

At National Geographic, we believe in adventure. We've spent over 100 years telling the stories of people who went somewhere they hadn't been before, people who had ideas that others hadn't had yet, people who embraced challenges, even looked for them.

Some adventurers just want to test themselves or want to get there first. George Mallory set out to climb Mount Everest " because it was there." Some adventurers want to find out more about the world. Primatologist Jane Goodall has spent most of her life in the forests of Tanzania, watching chimpanzees and learning more about them than anyone else ever has. Paul Sereno combs the world looking for fossil dinosaurs–evidence of a past as exciting as our present.

But adventure doesn't have to be so dramatic. Every time you climb a new tree, learn a new sport, make a new friend, or have a new idea, you're embarking on an adventure. Every time you decide to learn or discover something you didn't know before, you're having an adventure.

Some adventurers bring a lot of equipment with them. Some bring a little. But one thing that every adventurer carries is a journal. It's important to write down your new experiences so that you can look back on them later and share them with others.

This book is filled with quotes from adventurers and photographs of their adventures. And there's lots of space for you to write about your adventures and paste in your pictures. So go ahead and explore–your world, your head, and your heart. You'll be amazed what you find.

"The night… over the Pacific was a night of stars. They seemed to rise from the sea and hang outside my cockpit window, near enough to touch, until hours later they slipped away into the dawn."

—Amelia Earhart

Aviatrix

Date:

Adventure:

Date:

Adventure:

Date:

Adventure:

Date:

Adventure:

"Expeditions to the four corners of the Earth. Who could ask for anything more?"

–Paul Sereno

Dinosaur Paleontologist

Date:

Adventure:

Date:

Adventure:

"Gales and rain sailors take in stride,
but coupled with loneliness, they wear you down.
There's a limit to what you can take, getting knocked
about in a cockleshell with only a tape recorder to
converse with and a mad cat to yell at."

—Robin Lee Graham
Teenager who sailed the world alone

Date:

Adventure:

Date:

Adventure:

Date:

Adventure:

14

Date:

Adventure:

"Living in the Mir space station was like living
in the camper in the back of your pickup…
when it's raining and no one can get out."

–Shannon Lucid

Astronaut

Date: ....

Adventure: ....

....

....

....

....

....

....

....

....

....

....

....

....

....

....

....

....

....

....

Date:

Adventure:

Date:

Adventure:

Date:

Adventure:

"It was one thing to have won—
to have found the ship.
It was another thing to be there.
That was the spooky part. I could see the *Titanic*
as she slipped nose first into the glassy water."

–Robert D. Ballard
Undersea Explorer

Date:

Adventure:

Date:

Adventure:

"I was frequently scared and often tired but there were few moments I would have willingly missed."

–Sir Edmund Hillary
Mountain Climber

"We look up. For weeks, for months, that is all we have done. Look up. And there it is—the top of Everest. Only it is different now: so near, so close, only a little more than a thousand feet above us."

–Tenzing Norgay
Mountain Climber

Date:

Adventure:

Date:

Adventure:

Date:

Adventure:

Date:

Adventure:

Date:

Adventure:

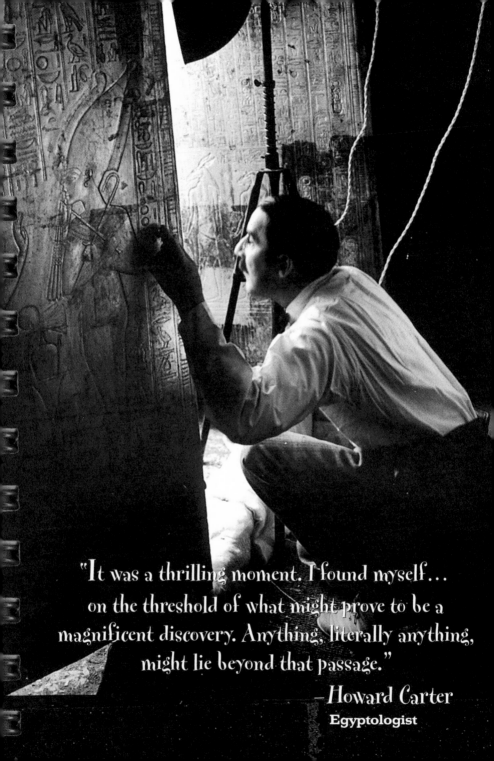

"It was a thrilling moment. I found myself...
on the threshold of what might prove to be a
magnificent discovery. Anything, literally anything,
might lie beyond that passage."

—Howard Carter
Egyptologist

Date:

Adventure:

Date:

Adventure:

"Sometimes I feel more at home underground than on the surface!"

–Nancy Holler Aulenbach

Cave Explorer

"I've been in caving passages no one has ever stepped in before. It's an overpowering emotion of exploration."

–Hazel A. Barton

Cave Explorer

Date:

Adventure:

Date:

Adventure:

Date:

Adventure:

"Whatever Lucy read in my eyes clearly satisfied her, for she suddenly put one arm around my neck and gave me a generous and very chimp-like kiss."

–Jane Goodall
Chimpanzee Researcher

Date:

Adventure:

Date:

Adventure:

Date:

Adventure:

Date:

Adventure:

"Do what you can do and don't let people push you back."
—Bessie Coleman

Aviatrix

Date:

Adventure:

Date:

Adventure:

Date:

Adventure:

"I've read that I flew up the hills and mountains of France. But you don't fly up a hill. You struggle slowly and painfully…and maybe, if you work very hard, you get to the top ahead of everybody else."

–Lance Armstrong
Bicyclist

Date:

Adventure:

Date:

Adventure:

Date:

Adventure:

"I dreamt… that some day I would go to the region of ice and snow and go on and on till I came to one of the poles of the earth, the end of the axis upon which this great ball turns."

–Ernest Shackleton
Antarctic Explorer

Date:

Adventure:

Date:

Adventure:

Date:

Adventure:

Date:

Adventure:

Date:

Adventure:

"In archaeology, you almost never find what you set out to find."

–Mary D. Leakey
Paleoanthropologist

Date:

Adventure:

Date:

Adventure:

Date:

Adventure:

"At age 17...
I strapped on my scuba gear...
balanced on the stern of a boat...
took a deep breath and jumped,
and that jump changed my life forever."

–Sylvia Earle

Marine Biologist and Ocean Explorer

Date:

Adventure:

Date:

Adventure:

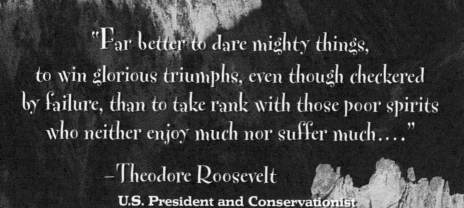

"Far better to dare mighty things,
to win glorious triumphs, even though checkered
by failure, than to take rank with those poor spirits
who neither enjoy much nor suffer much...."

–Theodore Roosevelt
U.S. President and Conservationist

Date:

Adventure:

Date:

Adventure:

Date:

Adventure:

Date:

Adventure:

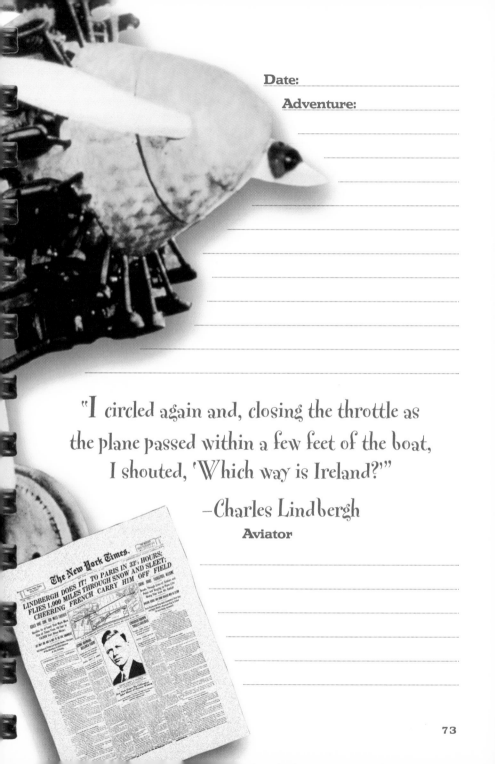

Date:

Adventure:

"I circled again and, closing the throttle as
the plane passed within a few feet of the boat,
I shouted, 'Which way is Ireland?'"

–Charles Lindbergh
Aviator

Date:

Adventure:

Date:

Adventure:

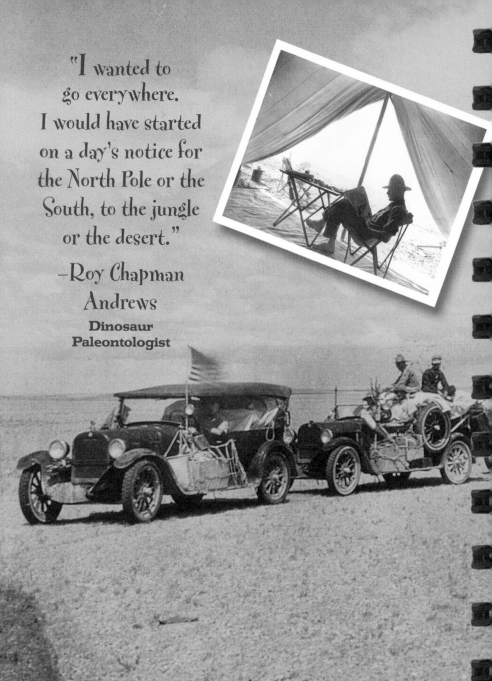

"I wanted to
go everywhere.
I would have started
on a day's notice for
the North Pole or the
South, to the jungle
or the desert."

–Roy Chapman
Andrews

**Dinosaur
Paleontologist**

Date: ....

Adventure: ....

....

....

....

....

....

....

....

....

....

Date:

Adventure:

Date:

Adventure:

"It was afternoon of the same day.
My flight had lasted just four hours and 56 minutes.
But I had seen three sunsets and three days,
flying from one day into the next and back again.
Nothing felt the same."

—John Glenn
Astronaut

Date:

Adventure:

Date:

Adventure:

Date:

Adventure:

Date:

Adventure:

Date:

Adventure:

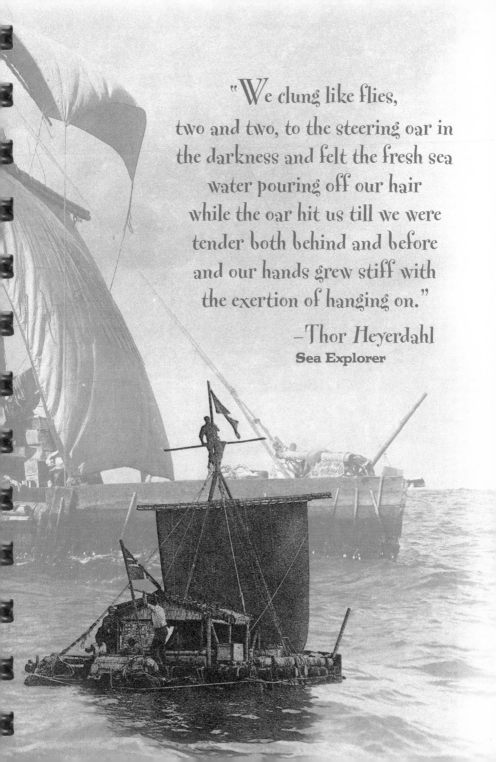

"We clung like flies,
two and two, to the steering oar in
the darkness and felt the fresh sea
water pouring off our hair
while the oar hit us till we were
tender both behind and before
and our hands grew stiff with
the exertion of hanging on."

–Thor Heyerdahl
Sea Explorer

Date:

Adventure:

Date:

Adventure:

Addresses

Addresses

name

address

phone

e-mail

name

address

phone

e-mail

name

address

phone

e-mail

name

address

phone

e-mail

Addresses

name

address

phone

e-mail

name

address

phone

e-mail

name

address

phone

e-mail

name

address

phone

e-mail

Addresses

name
....

address
....

....

phone
....

e-mail
....

name
....

address
....

....

phone
....

e-mail
....

name
....

address
....

....

phone
....

e-mail
....

name
....

address
....

....

phone
....

e-mail
....

Addresses

name
....

address
....

....

phone
....

e-mail
....

name
....

address
....

....

phone
....

e-mail
....

name
....

address
....

....

phone
....

e-mail
....

name
....

address
....

....

phone
....

e-mail
....

Addresses

name

address

phone

e-mail

name

address

phone

e-mail

name

address

phone

e-mail

name

address

phone

e-mail

Addresses

name
_____

address
_____

_____

phone
_____

e-mail
_____

name
_____

address
_____

_____

phone
_____

e-mail
_____

name
_____

address
_____

_____

phone
_____

e-mail
_____

name
_____

address
_____

_____

phone
_____

e-mail
_____

Addresses

name

address

phone

e-mail

name

address

phone

e-mail

name

address

phone

e-mail

name

address

phone

e-mail

Addresses

name

address

phone

e-mail

name

address

phone

e-mail

name

address

phone

e-mail

name

address

phone

e-mail

Addresses

name
....

address
....

....

phone
....

e-mail
....

name
....

address
....

....

phone
....

e-mail
....

name
....

address
....

....

phone
....

e-mail
....

name
....

address
....

....

phone
....

e-mail
....

Biographies

Biographies

ROY CHAPMAN ANDREWS, 1884–1960

When Roy Andrews graduated from college in 1906, he already knew he wanted to explore the natural world. He headed straight for the American Museum of Natural History in New York, where he cleaned floors just to work there. He didn't wash floors for long. Soon, he was sent on special assignments for the museum. In 1914, he went to Asia to collect animal specimens. There, he became convinced that the

deserts of Inner Mongolia might hold fossils of early dinosaurs, early humans, or both. In 1921, he and a team of scientists set out on one of the most astounding dinosaur excavations ever. Between 1921 and 1930, they unearthed 380 new species of living and fossilized animals and plants, including the skeleton of an *Oviraptor* sitting on her clutch of eggs. The team braved sand storms, irritable camels, poisonous snakes, local bandits, and hours of tedious digging and cataloging. When Andrews finally returned home, he became director of the museum where he had once washed floors. A fearless adventurer, many believe he was the model for the movie character Indiana Jones.

LANCE ARMSTRONG, 1972–

The people in Lance Armstrong's hometown of Plano, Texas, laughed whenever they saw him in his tight Lycra biking shorts. Boys simply didn't wear such things. Lance ignored the remarks about his clothes, his single mom, and their lack of money. By 16 he had decided that cycling would be his ticket out of Plano, and he was right. Disciplined and built to bike over long distances, Armstrong trained seven or eight hours a day. When he was 24, he won the World Champion-ship and one stage of the Tour de France (a three-week race over thousands of miles). But within a year, instead of being one of the world's top cyclists, he was

a cancer patient, diagnosed with a particularly lethal form of testicular cancer. After several surgeries and aggressive chemotherapy, which made him terribly sick, Lance's blood finally tested normal. By 1997 he was back on his bike. In 1999, just three years after learning about the cancer, he won the Tour de France. A year later, he won again, and then followed that victory with a bronze medal at the Olympics in Sydney, Australia.

Biographies

NANCY HOLLER AULENBACH, 1973–

For caver Nancy Holler Aulenbach, a 27-year-old elementary school teacher from Norcross, Georgia, being small is a definite asset. Her petite body frame allows her to squeeze into areas impossible for many other adults to reach. Born into a caving family, she made her first trip into the Earth when she was just a few months old, and she's being going underground ever since. She is an expert in descending sheer vertical pits, mapping complex labyrinths, and making daring cave rescues. When she's not teaching school, she works as a National Cave Rescue instructor. Today, her explorations take her all over the world, including ice caves in Greenland, underwater caves beneath the Yucatán jungles, and cliff caves above the Grand Canyon.

ROBERT D. BALLARD, 1942–

Bob Ballard, a National Geographic Explorer-in-Residence, has always been fascinated by the sea. When growing up in San Diego, he would wander the beaches, where every tide brought in something wonderful to examine. He followed his love of the sea all the way to a Ph.D. and then joined the Navy's Deep Submergence Laboratory. In 1977, he and his team were astounded to discover bizarre white crabs and six-foot-long worms that lived near hot vents on the ocean floor. How did these strange life-forms survive in such harsh conditions and how could he study them more closely? In his efforts to answer these questions, Ballard pioneered the use of sophisticated underwater search equipment, including an underwater robot he named Jason. Ballard's most famous find was the wreckage of the luxury ocean liner *Titanic*, which sank in the North Atlantic in 1912. Since that 1985 expedition, he has continued to search, successfully, for exotic life-forms and sunken ships. In 1989, Ballard formed the JASON Project, a program devoted to sharing the thrills of his scientific adventures with young students around the world by hooking them up via satellite to the actual robots he uses to search the ocean floor. Some kids even have a chance to run the controls.

HAZEL A. BARTON, 1972–

An Outward-Bound course that she took as a teenager in Bristol, England, hooked Hazel Barton on caving for life. Her first explorations took her into the muddy, wet limestone caves of England and Wales. Later, while a graduate student at the University of Colorado in Boulder, she began exploring all sorts of underground places—cliff caves that required serious rock climbing skills, underwater caves that required scuba diving, ice caves that demanded spiked boots, long ropes, and considerable courage. Her second great interest is animal diseases, which led her to a career in microbiology. Now she combines both as she explores the unusual ecosystems she finds deep underground. She believes that the organisms that can live in these extreme environments may provide insights into forms of life on other planets or point the way to new drugs and new forms of treatment for medical problems on this planet.

HOWARD CARTER, 1873–1939

For six years, Egyptologist Howard Carter dug through the rocks of Egypt's Valley of the Kings without success. Records indicated that a young pharaoh named King

Tutankhamen may have been buried there, but nothing had ever been found. The tombs of 27 other pharaohs buried in the Valley had been discovered and plundered centuries earlier. Was it possible that one last tomb lay untouched? Carter could only dream and dig. Then, on November 4, 1922, as Carter walked to the work site, he noticed a strange silence among the laborers. Beneath some simple huts, the men had found one limestone step. To protect against thievery, the ancient Egyptians hid the entrances to these tombs so the great treasure within would remain undetected. A step hinted at a stairway, which hinted at a chamber. The laborers uncovered step after step until the twelfth step brought them to a sealed doorway. Within, Carter found the tomb of King "Tut." It was the most intact Egyptian tomb of a pharaoh ever discovered, complete with a splendid burial chamber and rooms piled high with beautiful objects. Howard Carter brought the pharaoh and the time in which he lived to life and made the young king a household name more than 3,000 years after his death.

Biographies

BESSIE COLEMAN, 1893–1926

Bessie Coleman first heard of women flying airplanes when her brother returned from serving in World War I in Europe. As one of nine children in a poor, single-parent, Texas family, Bessie loved to hear tales of people defying the odds. She was determined to do so, too. And Bessie wanted to be a pilot. Because she was African American, no American school would give her flying lessons. Bessie took French lessons, earned enough money to get to Europe, and took her flying lessons in France. She returned with a piloting license, worked as a stunt pilot, and was immensely popular. Hoping to start a flying school for African Americans, she bought a run-down World War I flyer in 1926. It crashed during a practice run, killing both her and the mechanic, who was at the controls. Thousands mourned the death of "Queen Bess," as many called her. Every year on April 30, the anniversary of her death, members of the Bessie Coleman Aviators Club in Chicago fly over her grave to drop flowers in tribute to the lady who helped open the skies to minorities and women.

AMELIA EARHART, 1897–1937

Amelia Earhart saw her first plane at the 1908 Iowa State Fair when she was 11, but found the Ferris wheel more interesting. A decade later, while nursing pilots wounded in World War I, she became fascinated with their stories of aerial exploits. During off hours she'd go to a local runway where many of her former patients trained to watch them take off in a great rush of noise and air. Just two years later, by her twenty-fifth birthday, she'd saved enough money to take lessons and buy her own plane. Earhart went on to set many records, including becoming the first woman to make a round-trip solo flight across the United States. She set a speed record at 181 miles per hour and in 1932 became the first woman to fly solo across the Atlantic, battling fog and ice on the wings of her plane before landing in an Irish farmer's cow field. Beloved by millions for her daring and earthy charm, people across the globe mourned when they heard the news of her disappearance in 1937. She was on the final leg of another record-breaking run as the first woman to fly around the world when she and her navigator, Fred Noonan, vanished into the Pacific Ocean.

Biographies

SYLVIA EARLE, 1935–

When her family moved from New Jersey to Florida near the Gulf of Mexico, Sylvia Earle, then age 12, thought her world had collapsed. She loved the creatures that lived in the woodland near their old home. To her surprise, she found another wild universe to explore—the ocean. After earning a Ph.D. from Duke University, she became intrigued with underwater exploration and worked hard to become an expert diver as well as a first-rate scientist. In 1970, she was chosen as part of a team of women scientists to live in an underwater lab in the Caribbean for two weeks. They cataloged dozens of previously unknown

forms of marine life. After that, Earle wanted to dive even deeper into the secrets of the oceans. In 1979, using a pressurized suit that looked like a space suit, Earle planted the U.S. flag on the ocean floor at a depth of 1,250 feet, the deepest untethered dive in history. In 1985, she went even deeper, to 3,000 feet, this time in a one-person sub. Earle, a National Geographic Explorer-in-Residence, continues to be an advocate for the protection of the oceans and all the creatures that live there.

JOHN GLENN, 1921–

John Glenn's dad wanted him to stay in New Concord, Ohio, after he graduated from high school so he could take over the family plumbing business, but after reading a government ad calling for volunteer pilots, John knew he would never be a plumber. By 1944 he was flying bombing missions over the Pacific Ocean. After World War II, he served in Korea and then as a test pilot for the military's most sophisticated new planes. Then came news that the Russians had launched the first space satellite, *Sputnik*. With typical enthusiasm, Glenn entered NASA's new space program. On February 20, 1962, he piloted the spacecraft Friendship 7, becoming the first American to orbit the Earth. He returned home to an adoring public and a parade in New York City that drew four million people. In 1964 he ran for the Senate in Ohio and served as Senator for 35 years. Before retiring from public life, he went on yet another space adventure with the Space Shuttle Discovery in 1998, becoming the oldest astronaut to journey into outer space.

Biographies

JANE GOODALL, 1934–

When she was little, Jane Goodall decided to see if a chicken could actually produce an egg. For five hours, she sat in a neighbor's henhouse, waiting for the big drop. That was the beginning of an interest in science that has never ended. With no money for college, she had to put aside her dream of becoming a scientist. Instead, she followed a different dream, that of traveling to Africa to see the amazing animals there. While staying with a friend in Kenya, she met Dr. Louis Leakey, who hired her first to help him and then to lead a study of chimpanzees. He thought their behavior might shed light on life among prehistoric peoples, his main interest. In 1960 Goodall arrived on the shores of Lake Tanganyika in Tanzania to begin her work. The first few months were awful. The chimps ran away when her group approached, and she contracted malaria. After almost six months, she went into the jungle alone and just sat quietly. The chimps began watching her. She realized that, if alone, she might win their trust. She did and spent 30 years observing and sharing with the world the behavior of these endangered and endearing animals. Jane Goodall is now a National Geographic Explorer-in-Residence.

ROBIN LEE GRAHAM, 1949–

While on a year-long sail in the South Seas with his family, 13-year-old Robin Lee Graham learned to sail the ocean and navigate with a sextant. Three years later, he wanted to try an ocean journey alone. After considering the risks, he and his parents finally purchased a 24-foot sloop, *The Dove*. Graham planned a 22-day voyage from Los Angeles to Hawaii. On July 27, 1965, he headed west, with two kittens for company. The sail to Honolulu went so well that he wanted to go on, maybe even to circle the Earth. Over the next years, Graham braved hurricanes, broken masts at sea, a near-collision with a freighter, and depressing bouts of loneliness. He also landed on splendid islands where the inhabitants welcomed him with feasts. When he reached Barbados, in the Caribbean, he stopped. His boat was not strong enough to go on. After debating whether to continue, he finally bought a larger boat and set out again. On April 30, 1970, five years after he had begun, he sailed into Los Angeles, becoming the youngest person ever to sail around the world.

Biographies

THOR HEYERDAHL, 1914–

Norwegian explorer Thor Heyerdahl first heard the stories from an old man on a remote Pacific Island. Many islanders believed their ancestors had come from South America, across 4,000 miles of open sea, thousands of years earlier. Was that possible? Heyerdahl had seen pictures of raft-like vessels that ancient Peruvians had used.

Perhaps if he built such a raft and rode the currents and winds from South America to the Pacific Islands, he could prove that it was possible. After years of planning, Heyerdahl and a crew of six set off from the coast of Peru on a primitive raft named the *Kon-Tiki*. One hundred and one days later, the raft landed on a remote South-Sea island. It could be done, using only the resources Peruvians had available thousands of years ago. From then on, Heyerdahl continued to explore how ancient peoples traveled by sea, always questioning accepted theories by trying the voyages himself or poring over records to see what they would reveal about travels that scientists never imagined possible.

SIR EDMUND HILLARY, 1919–

When Edmund Hillary and the Sherpa Tenzing Norgay became the first humans known to reach the summit of Mount Everest on May 29, 1953, the whole world knew their names overnight. Hillary, a New Zealander and considered a British subject, was hailed as a national hero in England (as well as New Zealand) and knighted by the country's new queen, Elizabeth II. His celebrity was a surprise. His expertise as a mountain climber was not. He had spent years climbing in places like Mount Cook in New Zealand, the Swiss Alps, and other mountains in the Himalayan range. When the British decided to send an expedition to Mount Everest, Hillary, a beekeeper by profession, was a natural pick for the team. An enormous train of porters and other mountaineers were vital to Hillary's success, but it was his own strength and focus that allowed him to persevere. Hillary, always modest, added to his achievement when he used his fame to

build schools, hospitals, and other facilities to improve the lives of Sherpas living at the base of Everest and to help found a national park to protect the area.

Biographies

MARY LEAKEY, 1913–1996

Louis Leakey needed drawings for his book *Adam's Ancestors*, and he had heard that Mary Nicol was very good at sketching flint tools and skeleton remains. What began with pictures, ended with marriage, three children, and an astounding partnership that resulted in some of the most important fossil discoveries of early humans. After their marriage in 1936, they returned to Africa and their life's work. In 1948, Mary found the perfectly preserved 16-million-year-old skull of *Preconsul Africanus*, an early link to humans. In 1959, she found the skull of *Zinjanthropus*, a hominid that made tools. In 1978, a team led by Mary at Laetoli, in Tanzania, unearthed 3.5-million-year-old fossilized footprints of *Australopithecus*, which proved this now extinct cousin of man did indeed walk upright. While her discoveries made big news, it took years of careful work to find them. Mary and Louis spent hours sifting through dirt for even the smallest fragment from the past. Like her famous husband, Mary loved the mystery, the sense of discovery, and the joy that came every time they added another piece to the incomplete story of our origins.

CHARLES LINDBERGH, 1902–1974

Charles Lindbergh always thought he would be a farmer just like his Swedish ancestors, but his love of machines drew him to planes. In 1925 he graduated from flying

school and took a job as an airmail courier for the St. Louis-to-Chicago route. During the many lonely hours aloft, he began to imagine himself flying across the Atlantic. A Frenchman had offered $25,000 to the first pilot who could make the crossing. Even though several men had died trying, Lindbergh was sure he could do it. He thought their planes had been too heavy. Lindbergh convinced several St. Louis businessmen to loan him money for a new plane and then spent months looking for a manufacturer willing to work with an unknown pilot. Lindbergh took off from New York on May 20, 1927, in *The Spirit of St. Louis*. During the flight he had trouble staying oriented and awake. He had never flown over a large body of water before, nor for so long at one time. But 33½ hours after takeoff, he landed in Paris. Thousands rushed his plane. The era of modern air transportation had arrived.

Biographies

SHANNON LUCID, 1943–

After 188 days on board the space station *Mir* with two Russian astronauts, Shannon Lucid wasn't sure if she'd be able to stand when she returned to Earth. She had unintentionally set an American record for most days in space and a world record for space endurance for a woman astronaut because mechanical problems and terrible weather had delayed her return. When the capsule splashed down on September 26, 1996, she walked out, a bit wobbly, but all smiles. Shannon Lucid was well prepared to be an astronaut. Growing up in China with missionary par-

ents, she often experienced disruption and hardship. After her family moved to Oklahoma, she could pursue her two passions: science (she earned a doctorate in biochemistry) and flying (she also earned a pilot's license). When NASA chose an all-male team for the Mercury 7 project in the 1960s, Shannon decided it was time America had women astronauts. Accepted by NASA in 1978, Shannon represented the new space program—which put less emphasis on military pilots charging into space and more on scientific research. By the time she hooked up with *Mir* in 1996, she had already logged five missions and was the most experienced astronaut on NASA's staff, male or female.

TENZING NORGAY, 1914–1986

At 6:30 in the morning on May 29, 1953, Edmund Hillary and Tenzing Norgay set out for the final push to the top of Mount Everest, the highest mountain on land. Norgay had come within 813 feet of the summit the previous year, thus establishing himself as

an expert climber. A Sherpa whose countrymen live at the base of Mount Everest, Norgay first worked for years as a porter carrying other climbers' equipment. But he aspired to more and kept pushing to be included as a guide on ever higher climbs. After his success in 1953, he became internationally renowned. He and Hillary used much of the money they gained from their fame to fund the Mount Everest Foundation, which helps finance expeditions. In 1954 Norgay became director of the Himalayan Mountaineering Institute in Darjeeling, India, which trains climbers and guides. He died May 9, 1986, marking the end of a remarkable 72-year journey from his remote hometown in Nepal to the top of the world.

Biographies

THEODORE ROOSEVELT, 1858–1919

Theodore Roosevelt had such severe asthma as a child that he had to be tutored at his home rather than attend school. His father encouraged vigorous physical exercise to improve the boy's health, and it worked. Roosevelt was even on the boxing team at Harvard University. After college, he married and began what became a lifetime of work in government. Then tragedy struck. Both his mother and his wife died on the same day. Grief-stricken, he headed west where he worked as a cowboy and rancher. Two years later, he returned to the East and to government. In 1901, he became President of the United States. Roosevelt knew that the wildlife he loved in the West wouldn't last long if the government didn't protect it. He used the power of his office to set aside acres and acres of land for conservation and public enjoyment. During his two terms as president, he established 150 National Forests, 5 National Parks, and 55 bird and game preserves. He also pushed legislation through Congress that provided special protection for 18 natural landmarks, including the Grand Canyon.

PAUL SERENO, 1958–

Paul Sereno grew up in Naperville, Illinois, a mischievous, underachieving boy who struggled in school. Then, on a field trip with his brother to the American Museum of Natural History in New York City, the drifty teenager found something to focus on. He fell in love with everything the museum had—the displays, the stories of adventure, and more. He went on to study paleontology at Columbia University and became famous for unearthing one incredible find after another. After three weeks on his first major dig in Argentina in 1988, Sereno found the fossilized remains of a nearly complete *Herrerasaurus*, the best

preserved specimen ever discovered. Just three years later he made an even more incredible discovery: the fossilized remains of an *Eoraptor*, the most primitive dinosaur ever found. In 1993, he began work in the Sahara in Africa. There, too, he has made one spectacular discovery after another. Thanks to his amazing finds, Sereno, a National Geographic Explorer-in-Residence, is often called the superstar of contemporary paleontology, a kind of Roy Chapman Andrews of our time.

Biographies

SIR ERNEST SHACKLETON, 1874–1922

Ernest Shackleton failed in every expedition he ever led. He never reached the South Pole or crossed the Antarctic continent, as he had set out to do. Yet he was a hero by any standard. An Irish boy from a large family, Shackleton began his career as a lowly seaman in the British merchant marine. But he proved that he had the good humor and iron resolve that inspired those who worked with him. In 1915 he set out on the ship *Endurance* for Antarctica, where he and 27 other men planned to walk the 1,500 miles across the continent. But the *Endurance* became trapped in the ice floes around Antarctica, and the men could do nothing but watch the slow-moving ice crush the hull of their ship. Stranded hundreds of miles from the closest outpost, many in the party thought they had no chance. Not Shackleton. He led his men from ice floe to ice floe, dragging boats and what supplies they had with them. When they finally reached land—the desolate Elephant Island—he left the bulk of the group while he and five other men set off in a 22-foot lifeboat to make the 700-mile crossing to a whaling station on the island of South Georgia. For days they faced bitter cold seas, enormous waves, horrible thirst, and near starvation. It took 17 days to reach the island and 24 more hours to reach the camp. Concerned for the safety of the 22 men left behind, Shackleton spent just one day recovering before setting off again in a ship to pick up his crew. All survived, thanks to their captain's indomitable spirit and bold actions.

A Map of Adventure

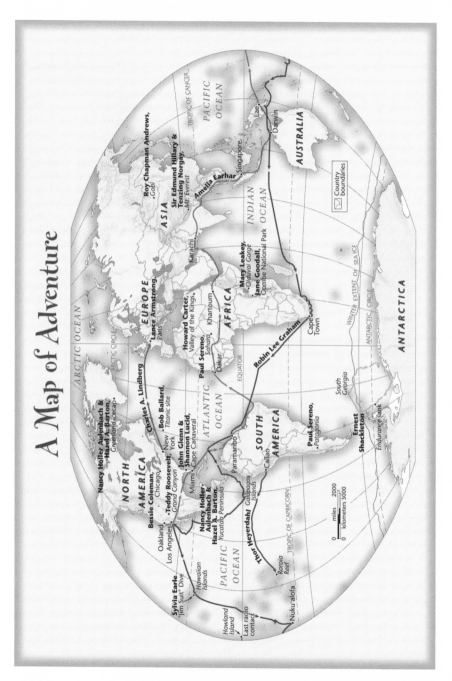

That's Adventure

The adventurers featured in this journal explored
and studied and lived all over the world, as you
can see on the map. They were on every continent,
on the tallest mountains, in the deepest seas,
high in the air, under ground, and even in space.
They followed their curiosity, their longing for
challenge, their need to explore and learn
and try all they could.

Now, you have done much the same. You've just
filled this journal with all your adventures. Time
to get a new journal and start again. There's
always an adventure just ahead.

BEWARE

TYRANNOSAURUS

AHEAD

Published by the National Geographic Society

John M. Fahey, Jr., *President and Chief Executive Officer*

Gilbert M. Grosvenor, *Chairman of the Board*

Nina D. Hoffman, *Executive Vice-President, President of Books and School Publishing*

Staff for This Book

Nancy Laties Feresten, *Publishing Director, Children's Books*

Bea Jackson, *Art Director, Children's Books*

Jo H. Tunstall, *Project Editor*

NewEarthMedia, *Design*

Janet Dustin, *Illustrations Editor*

Mary Collins, *Writer*

Joseph F. Ochlak, *Map Research*

Jerome N. Cookson, *Map Production*

Melissa Farris, *Design Assistant*

Lewis R. Bassford, *Production Manager*

Vincent P. Ryan, *Manufacturing Manager*